Feelings

UNDERSTANDING OUR FEELINGS OF SADNESS, HAPPINESS, LOVE & LONELINESS

By **Mary Anne McElmurry**

Illustrated by **Darcy Tom**

Copyright © Good Apple, Inc. 1981

ISBN NO. 0-86653-027-4

GOOD APPLE, INC.
BOX 299
CARTHAGE, IL 62321

Description of Kino Learning Center

Kino Learning Center is a private, nonprofit Catholic elementary school founded in 1975 by parents seeking an alternative learning environment for children. The school is staffed by 30 teachers and has an enrollment of 300 students between the ages of 3 and 18.

At Kino Learning Center the students, teachers, and parents form a learning community in which people are bound together in mutual aid, responsibility, and cooperation. Freedom exists within this interaction as the liberty persons grant to each other out of their faith in and concern for one another. Such freedom is nourished by mutual respect and appreciation; from it, trust grows and individuality flourishes.

Within the prepared learning environment of the school, each child is free to choose from worthwhile options, a sequence of activities unique to his/her needs and experiences, and in which he/she finds success, interest, and pleasure. Each child is free to develop in the way and at the pace appropriate to his/her needs, abilities, and interests. The school places special stress on individual discovery, on firsthand experience, and on creative work.

At Kino Learning Center, adults and children mutually engaged in the learning process are continually in the process of changing and growing, for to learn is to change. And to experience joy in learning is to delight in life itself, for learning and life are one.

Dedication

To the Kino teachers: in gratitude for your
feelings of love and compassion.

Acknowledgements

Special thanks to Judy Bisignano, Mary Jane Cera, and Linda Brawner whose FEELINGS for children and their learning styles have helped make this book possible.

This book is partially funded by a grant from the Raskob Foundation (Wilmington, Delaware).

Introduction

Many critics of modern society point to the loss of a sense of values as a major cause of contemporary problems. While the blame is often placed on the young and teenaged, all age levels seem to have shifted away from an awareness of where they are going. Today's youth are highly criticized for a behavior which reflects a lack of respect for self-and others; a general disregard for people and things. There is a drastic need for adult America to assist its youth to deal with the innumerable areas of confusion and conflict in our modern society. The need for the development of a positive self-image and a value system consistent with one's beliefs and behaviors is a vital part of one's existence and survival.

Values can best be developed through questioning one's own feelings and behaviors as well as discussing and responding to the feelings and behaviors of others. Values can also be developed through making decisions in an atmosphere that allows many choices, invites relevant questions, and encourages respect for self and others.

The development of values must be seen as a lifelong process which recognizes changing circumstances rather than a fixed set of unyielding principles. Rather than reacting to a predetermined, fixed moral code, youngsters must be encouraged to develop a self-determined value system which reflects a respect for self, others, and things.

It is the teachers of a school who set the tone and create the atmosphere that is so necessary and appropriate to value education. Their approach to life, their feelings and responses toward themselves and others, their attitudes toward all living things and the environment, have a profound influence upon the attitudes and behavior of their students. It is in this warm, accepting atmosphere that students are invited to develop a tolerance, acceptance, and genuine concern for themselves, others, and living and nonliving things.

Teachers must create innumerable activities and situations which, while developing skills in academic areas, at the same time lead a child toward a basic understanding and development of humaneness. Helping children to become concerned and actively involved in finding solutions to problems is an important aspect of value development.

The activities in this book are designed to assist students to develop a better understanding of and appreciation for their feelings of love, happiness, sadness, and loneliness by:

1) developing communication skills which maximize awareness of what they are experiencing and what they perceive others to be experiencing;

2) recognizing the values they presently hold and how these values may change as a result of new information and experiences; and

3) developing a behavior consistent with their basic attitudes and convictions about their feelings of love, happiness, sadness, and loneliness.

As the activities in this book are completed, students will have repeated opportunities to affirm each other's uniqueness, capability, and lovability. This need for a positive self-image, value code, and consistent beliefs and behaviors is vital for today's youth as they begin to hold a more constructive and positive view of themselves and their world. Herein lies the challenge of the present moment and the hope for all that is worthwhile for generations to come.

Feeling Love

Part One:
to identify my feelings of love.

Purpose:
The purpose of the activities in this book is to assist you in identifying your feelings of love, happiness, sadness, and loneliness.

Before beginning Part One, **Feeling Love**, complete the following statements:

	Always	Usually	Sometimes	Seldom	Never
1. I love myself	☐	☐	☐	☐	☐
2. I love people	☐	☐	☐	☐	☐
3. I love animals	☐	☐	☐	☐	☐
4. I show my love for people	☐	☐	☐	☐	☐
5. People show their love for me	☐	☐	☐	☐	☐

Name _____

Date _____

Kindness
Openness

1. Describing Love

Discuss with your teacher and classmates those words which describe **love**. Write the words in the letter L.

The dictionary defines love as

_____

_____

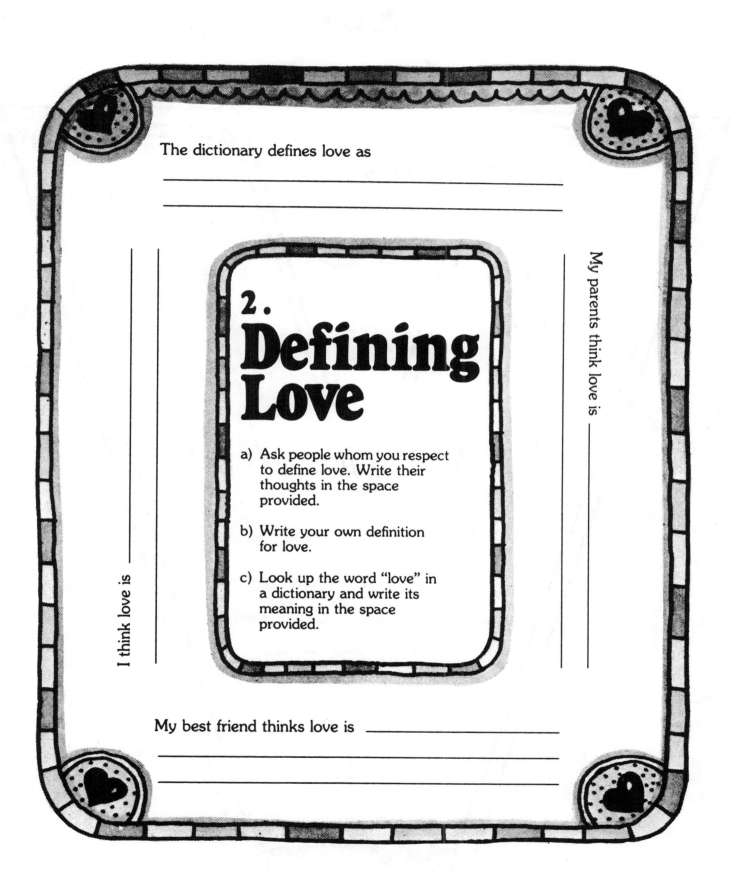

My parents think love is _____

I think love is _____

2.
Defining Love

a) Ask people whom you respect to define love. Write their thoughts in the space provided.

b) Write your own definition for love.

c) Look up the word "love" in a dictionary and write its meaning in the space provided.

My best friend thinks love is _____

_____

3. I Am Loved

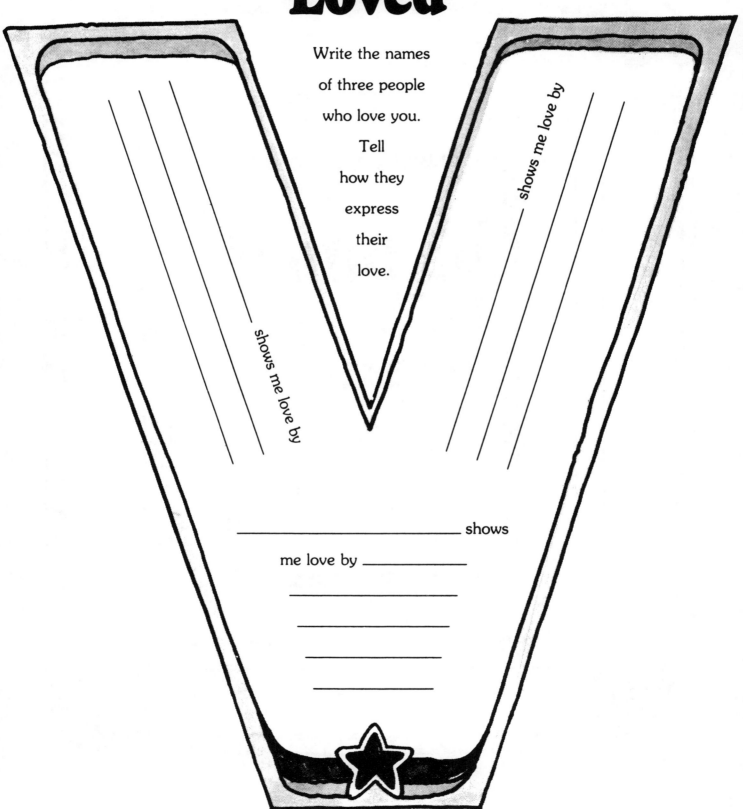

Write the names of three people who love you. Tell how they express their love.

shows me love by

shows me love by

_____ shows me love by _____

People I Love

_____
_____
_____
_____
_____
_____
_____

4. Loving People, Places, & Things

Write the names of people and things you love in the spaces provided. Write the name of a place that you especially love.

Things I Love

_____
_____
_____
_____
_____
_____
_____

A Place I Love _____

5. Love Poster

Cut out the letters L - O - V - E from Activities 1 through 4.
Glue the letters to a large sheet of construction paper
or poster board. Decorate your love poster. Hang your
poster in a special place in your home.

6. Secret Friend

Write the name of each person in the class on a small
piece of paper. Put the names in a box. Have each
person in the class draw one name from the box.

For one week, do loving things for the
person whose name you chose. Be careful
not to let your secret friend (or anyone
else) know who you are. At the end
of the week, have each person tell
of one loving thing that was done for
him/her. When your secret friend
describes a loving thing that you did,
let him/her know that you are
his/her secret friend.

7. Making a New Friend

Find a partner among your classmates whom you do not know very well. Discuss the following questions with each other:

a) How many brothers and sisters do you have?

b) Would you like to have more or fewer brothers and sisters? Why?

c) What is your favorite color?

d) Do you have a lucky number?

e) What is your favorite movie?

f) What is your favorite book?

g) What is your favorite T V show?

h) What do you like most about school?

i) What do you like least about school?

j) Do you have a hobby?

k) What are some things you enjoy doing?

l) What is the most exciting thing you have ever done?

m) What would you like to be able to do someday?

n) What is a wish that you hope comes true?

o) What do you worry about?

After the conversation, tell the class about one of the most important items your friend discussed with you.

8. Signing Love

This is the international sign language symbol for "I love you." Practice making this sign. Use the sign to share love with a deaf person or when greeting or leaving a friend.

9. I Love You

Learn to say "I love you" in at least three languages other than English. Write "I love you" in three different languages. For example,

German   Ich liebe Dich

_____   _____

_____   _____

_____   _____

10. Don't Forget Me!

Many older people who need special care live in nursing homes. Some people in nursing homes receive much care, but little love.

To show love to people in a nursing home, I could:

1. _____

2. _____

3. _____

4. _____

Visit a nursing home and show some older people that you care about them. Try to visit the home on a regular basis.

Tell about your experience below.

_____
_____
_____
_____
_____
_____
_____
_____
_____

11. Flying High

Listed below are colors that describe feelings of love and symbols that describe signs of love.

Decorate your kite with the colors and symbols that best describe your feelings of love.

COLORS

green - kindness
blue - forgiveness
red - helpfulness
yellow - gentleness
orange - happiness
purple - truthfulness

SYMBOLS

O = hugs
X = kisses
⌣ = smiles
△ = gifts
□ = spending time with a person
★ = giving compliments

12. **Nature Lover**

Make a list of the things in nature that you love.

Put a star (*) next to the three things in nature that you love most.

_____

_____

_____

_____

_____

_____

_____

_____

_____

_____

_____

_____

13. **Nature Collage**

Make a nature collage using pictures of things in nature you most love. Hang your nature collage in your classroom.

14. Animal Lover

a. Many people love animals because

_____

_____

_____

b. The animal I like most is _____

because _____

_____

_____

c. How can people show their love for animals by respecting their right to live?

_____

_____

_____

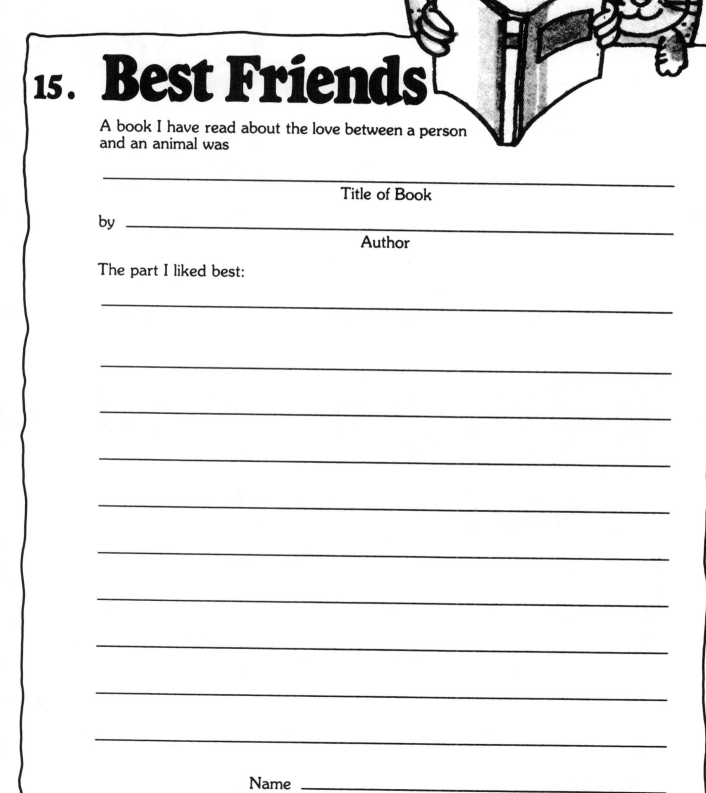

15. **Best Friends**

A book I have read about the love between a person and an animal was

_____

Title of Book

by _____

Author

The part I liked best:

_____

_____

_____

_____

_____

_____

_____

_____

_____

_____

_____

Name _____

16. Plants Need Love?

It has been said that plants respond to love.

To show love to a plant, I would:

a. _____

b. _____

c. _____

d. _____

Buy two identical plants. Treat both plants the same, except for one thing. Show frequent love to one plant. Do not show any love to the other plant. Observe the plants after a two-week period. Record your observations below.

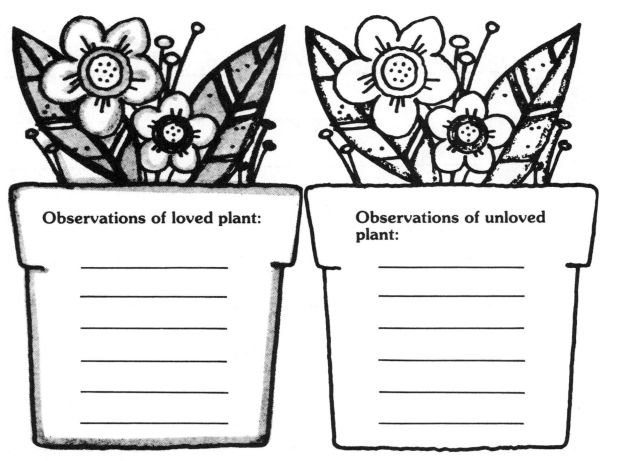

Observations of loved plant:

_____
_____
_____
_____
_____
_____

Observations of unloved plant:

_____
_____
_____
_____
_____
_____

Note: At the completion of this experiment, give the plants to someone you love very much.

17. Lack of Love

Describe a world without love.

18. Needing Love

Discuss with your teacher and classmates:

a. What would happen to you if you did not experience love in your life?

b. What you do to show that you want and need love.

19. Close Encounters

Imagine that you will soon be leaving on the first space shuttle to a distant planet. You will be able to bring only three people with you. Name these people. Tell why you would want each person to go with you on this long journey.

1. _____

_____

_____

_____

2. _____

_____

_____

3. _____

_____

_____

_____

20. Poetry Lover

Find or write a poem about love. Write the poem in the space provided. Illustrate your poem.

21. Love Receives

a. Name a special gift that you have received from someone who loves you.

b. What is the greatest gift that you have received from your parents?

_____

_____

Have you recently thanked your parents for this gift?

22. Love Letter

Write a letter to a special person in your life. Tell this person why you love him/her. Thank this person for his/her gift of love to you. Give or mail your letter to this person.

23. Gift of Love

Fill in the following gift certificates.
Cut them out and give them to people you love.
Give the gift stated on each certificate.

Sample:
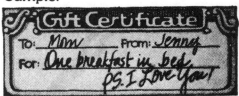

Gift Certificate

TO: _____ From: _____

For: _____

P.S. I Love You!

Gift Certificate

TO: _____ From: _____

For: _____

P.S. I Love You!

Gift Certificate

TO: _____ From: _____

For: _____

P.S. I Love You!

Summary: Feeling Love

The purpose of Part One of this book was to assist you in identifying your feeling of love. Summarize your thoughts in the space provided.

I love

_____

_____

_____

_____

Love is

_____

_____

_____

_____

_____

I am loved by

_____

_____

_____

_____

Colors and symbols
that depict love

A special gift of love
that I have received

_____

_____

_____

_____

from

_____

Check one:
After completing Part One,

	Always	Usually	Sometimes	Seldom	Never
1. I love myself	☐	☐	☐	☐	☐
2. I love people	☐	☐	☐	☐	☐
3. I love animals	☐	☐	☐	☐	☐
4. I show my love for people	☐	☐	☐	☐	☐
5. People show their love for me	☐	☐	☐	☐	☐

I can identify my feelings of love:

☐ more

☐ less

☐ about the same

Name _____

Date _____

Feeling Happiness

Part Two:
to describe my feelings of happiness.

Before beginning Part two, **Feeling Happiness**, complete the following statements:

	Always	Usually	Sometimes	Seldom	Never
1. I am happy	☐	☐	☐	☐	☐
2. I show my happiness	☐	☐	☐	☐	☐
3. Other people are happy	☐	☐	☐	☐	☐
4. Other people show their happiness	☐	☐	☐	☐	☐

Name _____

Date _____

24. Happy Times

I am happy when:

1. _____
2. _____
3. _____
4. _____
5. _____

Put a star (★) before the sentence that tells when you are **most** happy.

25. Year 'Round Happiness

Listed below are the four seasons of the year. What is something that happens in each of these seasons that makes you happy?

WINTER	**SPRING**	**SUMMER**	**FALL**
_____	_____	_____	_____
_____	_____	_____	_____

26. Happy People

The happiest person I know is . . .

I know that this person is
happy because

_____
_____
_____
_____
_____

NAME

27. Looking Happy

Look at yourself in a mirror.
Practice smiling and looking happy.
Remember how looking happy
feels. Try looking and feeling happy
many times throughout the day.

28. Happiness Survey

Ask four people to name three things that make them happy. Record their answers in the blossoms below. Cut out the blossoms and add them to the "Tree of Happiness" bulletin board in the classroom.

Name

Name

Name

Name

29. What's Important?

Many times we keep the things that we value near us. Our bedrooms are often our treasure boxes. List the things in your bedroom which you feel add to your happiness.

_____

_____

_____

_____

_____

_____

_____

_____

_____

_____

Star (★) the three things in your bedroom that bring you the most happiness. Could you keep your happiness if you were to lose these most important possessions?

_____

30. Keys to Happiness

Listed below are some possible ways to acquire happiness. Color those keys that are most important to you at this time.

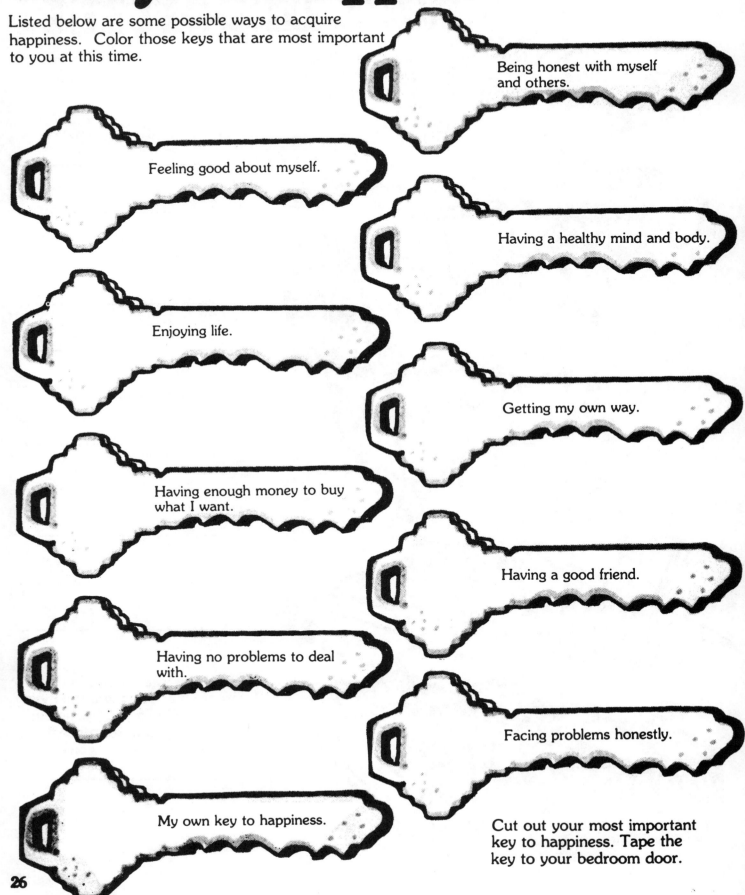

Being honest with myself and others.

Feeling good about myself.

Having a healthy mind and body.

Enjoying life.

Getting my own way.

Having enough money to buy what I want.

Having a good friend.

Having no problems to deal with.

Facing problems honestly.

My own key to happiness.

Cut out your most important key to happiness. Tape the key to your bedroom door.

31. Steps to Happiness

Listed below are the "keys to happiness" from Activity 30. Construct the stepladder to happiness by cutting out and gluing the least important means to happiness on the bottom rung of your ladder. Continue to climb the ladder by determining your priorities for happiness. The top rung of the ladder should indicate your most important means of happiness.

HAVING NO
PROBLEMS

FEELING GOOD
ABOUT MYSELF

HAVING A
GOOD FRIEND

BEING
HEALTHY

BEING
HONEST

FACING
PROBLEMS

HAVING
MONEY

GETTING MY
OWN WAY

ENJOYING
LIFE

Write your own
step to happiness

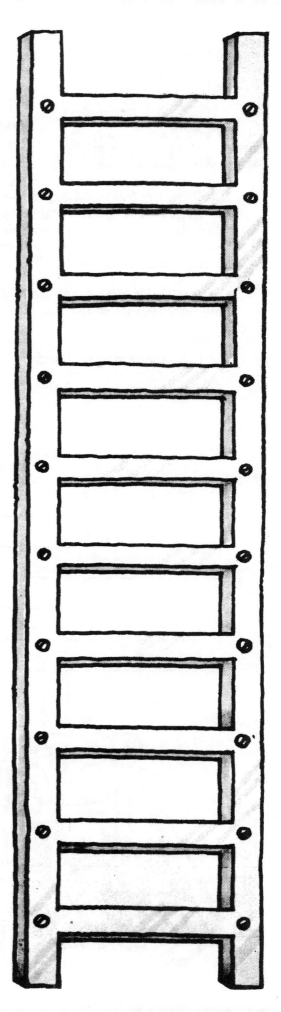

32. Think Happy

Perform the following experiment for one week. Before you get up in the morning, lie back and let your body relax. Make a mental list of happy thoughts. Let these thoughts pass through your mind. Say to yourself three times: "This is going to be a good day for me. I believe I can handle all problems. I feel good all over. It is wonderful to be alive."

Repeat this saying many times during the day. At the end of the day, think about the good points of the day.

At the end of seven days, evaluate the week to see if your choice to be happy actually made you feel and be happier.

State your evaluation below.

_____

_____

_____

_____

_____

_____

_____

_____

_____

33. Wish Upon a Star

Make five wishes for happiness and write them on the star. Discuss your wishes with your teacher and classmates. Cut out the star and pin it to the bulletin board entitled, "May Our Dreams Come True."

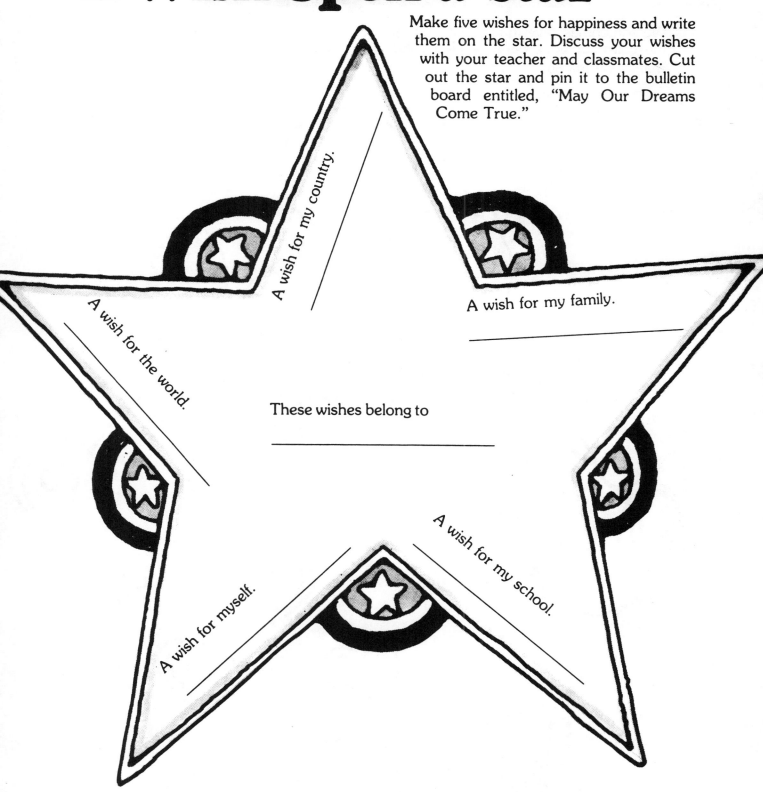

A wish for my country.

A wish for my family.

A wish for the world.

These wishes belong to

A wish for myself.

A wish for my school.

34. Saving Happiness

We sometimes save things that we hope will bring us happiness. Label the coins for your Bank of Happiness with the names of things that make you happy.

35. Sharing Happiness

Make a withdrawal from the Bank of Happiness.

Fill out the checks as shown in the sample. Cut out the checks and share your happiness with people who are important to you.

Sample:

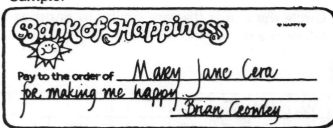

Bank of Happiness   ♡ HAPPY ♡

Pay to the order of _Mary Jane Cera_
for making me happy.

Brian Crowley

Bank of Happiness   ♡ HAPPY ♡

Pay to the order of _____

_____

_____

Bank of Happiness   ♡ HAPPY ♡

Pay to the order of _____

_____

_____

Bank of Happiness   ♡ HAPPY ♡

Pay to the order of _____

_____

_____

36. Word Find for Happiness

Circle the words that are similar to **happiness** in the word find below.
Work the puzzle with a friend.

W	B	T	K	P	L	A	Y	F	U	L	N	E	S	S	P
A	E	J	M	S	C	L	M	J	O	A	R	K	A	W	J
E	X	U	B	E	R	A	N	C	E	U	N	G	T	B	O
X	O	I	A	D	R	B	F	H	Z	G	V	L	J	O	Y
H	P	G	O	Q	H	G	L	E	E	H	S	A	Q	L	O
I	T	N	G	P	C	D	E	E	S	T	I	D	R	C	U
L	I	G	H	T	H	E	A	R	T	E	D	N	E	S	S
A	M	F	E	O	A	S	X	F	H	R	Z	E	J	Y	N
R	I	G	H	A	P	P	Y	U	B	K	D	S	O	H	E
A	S	Z	R	Y	P	J	O	L	L	Y	E	S	I	L	S
T	M	E	R	R	I	M	E	N	T	R	L	J	C	I	S
I	P	D	M	X	N	F	R	E	J	O	I	C	I	N	G
O	L	S	C	H	E	E	R	S	E	Q	G	T	N	O	S
N	O	R	U	M	S	W	Q	S	C	K	H	J	G	V	P
N	B	L	I	S	S	F	U	L	D	F	T	U	G	C	M

happiness	delight	rejoicing	exuberance
cheer	gladness	glee	happy
merriment	playfulness	joy	exhilaration
joyousness	cheerfulness	lightheartedness	blissful
laughter	optimism	zest	jolly

37. Appreciation Award

Fill in the medal of appreciation. Color and cut out the medal.
Give it to someone who brings you happiness.

38. Recipe for Happiness

Make your own recipe for happiness by determining the amounts and ingredients for happiness.
Complete the recipe below.

"Here's what's cookin'"
Happiness Recipe

39. Happy Poster

Make a happy poster with your favorite slogan that would put a smile on the face of the reader. Give your poster to a person who brings you happiness.

40. Level of Happiness

Color in the scale to the level that best indicates your general degree of happiness.

Discuss with your teacher and classmates:

a) why you believe you are at the indicated level of happiness,

b) how you might increase your level of happiness, and

c) how you might sustain your level of happiness.

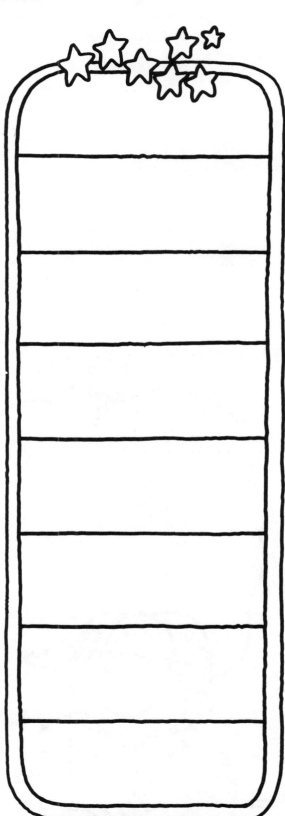

41. Future Dreams

List five things that you believe would add to your happiness in the future. Star (★) that item you believe would bring you the **most** happiness.

1. _____

2. _____

3. _____

4. _____

5. _____

Summary: Feeling Happiness

The purpose of Part Two of this book was to assist you in describing your feelings of happiness. Summarize your thoughts in the space provided.

People make me happy when _____
_____
_____

Happiness is _____
_____

One thing I own that I value a great deal

is _____

I am most happy when
_____
_____
_____

I show my happiness by
_____
_____
_____

I believe the key to happiness is
_____

A wish for happiness is
_____
_____
_____

The happiest person

I know is _____
_____

because _____
_____

Check One.
After completing Part Two,

	Always	Usually	Sometimes	Seldom	Never
1. I am happy	☐	☐	☐	☐	☐
2. I show my happiness	☐	☐	☐	☐	☐
3. Other people are happy	☐	☐	☐	☐	☐
4. Other people show their happiness	☐	☐	☐	☐	☐

I am aware of my feelings of happiness:

☐ more

☐ less

☐ about the same

Name _____

Date _____

Feeling Sad

Part Three:

to describe my feelings of sadness.

Before beginning Part Three, **Feeling Sad,** complete the following statements:

	Always	Usually	Sometimes	Seldom	Never
1. I feel sad	☐	☐	☐	☐	☐
2. I show that I feel sad	☐	☐	☐	☐	☐
3. People close to me feel sad	☐	☐	☐	☐	☐
4. People close to me show when they are sad	☐	☐	☐	☐	☐

Name _____

Date _____

42. Defining Sadness

Listed below are 10 words that are similar in meaning to **sadness**. Find and circle each word in the puzzle. Discuss the meaning of each word with your teacher and classmates.

downcast
glum
grieved
mournful
dejected
weep
joyless
sorrowful
heartbroken
depressed

V	T	I	U	Z	A	W	H	N	Y	M	W
S	R	K	H	M	G	O	P	X	V	O	X
C	G	J	L	S	Q	U	K	T	R	U	F
B	D	O	W	N	C	A	S	T	E	R	C
H	E	A	R	T	B	R	O	K	E	N	S
A	P	D	H	K	S	P	L	T	F	F	E
G	R	I	E	V	E	D	K	U	M	U	T
W	E	E	P	O	M	P	L	G	Q	L	N
J	S	F	Y	Z	J	E	D	L	B	C	A
B	S	O	R	R	O	W	F	U	L	D	D
Y	E	N	W	I	Y	E	F	M	C	O	C
Z	D	S	X	L	L	M	E	R	G	Q	P
K	F	G	H	D	E	J	E	C	T	E	D
M	P	O	N	H	S	K	K	H	B	I	G
B	O	I	J	T	S	J	A	U	L	J	V

40

43. Puzzling Faces

A. Facial expressions communicate feelings without using words.
Label these facial expressions using the terms below.

frown   grimace   pout   scowl   sneer

_____   _____   _____

_____   _____

B. Use a mirror to make the expressions above.
Describe a time when a person might frown, grimace, pout,
scowl or sneer.

44. Expressing Sadness

Use the words from Activity 43 to complete the statements and solve the puzzle.

frown
grimace
pout
scowl
sneer

ACROSS

1. A _____ expresses anger.
4. A _____ expresses pain.

DOWN

2. A _____ expresses sulkiness.
3. A _____ expresses sarcasm.
5. A _____ expresses meanness.

45. Finger Feelings

Make two finger paintings, one expressing how you feel when you are sad and one expressing how you feel when you are happy.

Feeling Sad   Feeling Happy

46. Causes for Sadness

Sadness is a choice. You allow yourself to feel sad.
Some situations in which you allow yourself to feel sad are

1. _____

2. _____

3. _____

4. _____

5. _____

47. Solutions for Sadness

Choose one situation in which you allow yourself to feel sad. Discuss with your teacher a plan of action to change your sadness to happiness. Try out your plan. After one week, discuss with your teacher the effectiveness of your plan.

48. Which Sadness is Saddest?

Listed below are some things that people can choose to feel sad about. Rearrange the list so that the item that feels the most sad to you is at the top and the item that feels the least sad is at the bottom. You may add other items that you feel sad about if they are not listed.

fight with friend

loss of valuable object

death of friend

punishment

physical disability

loss of pet

loneliness

old age

divorce of parents

hunger

_____

_____

1. _____

2. _____

3. _____

4. _____

5. _____

6. _____

7. _____

8. _____

9. _____

10. _____

11. _____

12. _____

49. Easing Sadness

Listed below are some things that people allow to be a cause of sadness. Explain how each item could be a reason for sadness and what you could do to lessen the sadness.

	Reason for sadness	What to do to lessen the sadness
Loneliness	_____ _____ _____	_____ _____ _____
Old Age	_____ _____ _____	_____ _____ _____
Divorce	_____ _____ _____	_____ _____ _____
Fighting	_____ _____ _____ _____	_____ _____ _____ _____

50. Causing My Own Sadness

There are some things about which we feel sad that we cannot control. For example, we cannot control a volcano that erupts and hurts many people.

We also feel sad about some things which we can control. For example, in our anger, we may hurt someone's feelings.

After a volcano and after hurting someone's feelings we may feel sad. We cannot control a volcano, but we can control our anger.

Categorize the following causes of sad situations into things that you can control and things that you cannot control. Add two items to each list.

rain   fear   fire
jealousy   death   fighting

Things I can control:

_____
_____
_____
_____
_____
_____

Things I cannot control:

_____
_____
_____
_____
_____

51. Actions in Sadness

What do you like to do when you feel sad?

_____ talk to a family member.

_____ talk to a friend.

_____ be alone in my room.

_____ go to a quiet spot outdoors.

_____ do some physical activity.

_____ other _____

_____

52. Taking a Poll

Ask five people what they allow to make them sad.
Ask these same people what they allow to make them happy.
Record your answers below.

Person	I am sad when . . .
1	
2	
3	
4	
5	

Person	I am happy when . . .
1	
2	
3	
4	
5	

Summarize the results of your poll below.

_____

_____

_____

53. In the News

Watch the news on television for one week. Count the number of happy news reports. Count the number of sad news reports. Keep track of the number of sad and happy reports on the graph below.

Happy News Events

Sad News Events

Summarize the results of your survey below.

_____

_____

_____

_____

_____

54. Reporting Sadness

Cut out an article from a newspaper or magazine that is a source of sadness for you. Discuss the article with your teacher and classmates. Tell why you have sad feelings from reading the article. Make up a happy ending for your story.

55. Headlining Happiness

Cut out a headline from a newspaper or magazine that is a source of sadness for you. On a strip of paper (4 in. x 24 in.), print a happy headline. Display your sad and happy headlines on a classroom bulletin board.

56. Looking on the Good Side

Often we allow sadness in our lives because we look at situations with a negative attitude. Change the following negative statements to positive statements:

Example: Fish smell bad.
            Fish taste better than they smell.

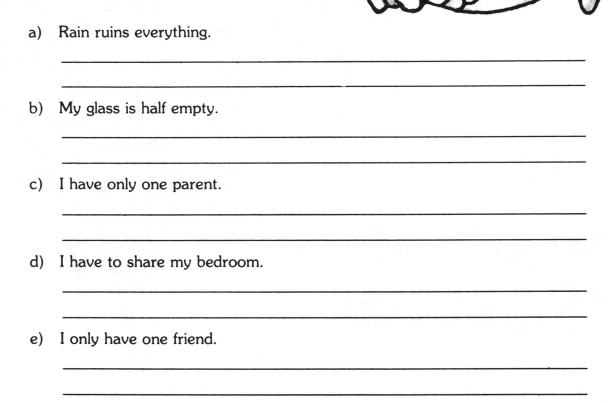

a)   Rain ruins everything.

_____

_____

b)   My glass is half empty.

_____

_____

c)   I have only one parent.

_____

_____

d)   I have to share my bedroom.

_____

_____

e)   I only have one friend.

_____

_____

57. Sad Isn't Always Bad

Think about a time in your life when you felt sad about something and later it turned out to be a happy experience for you. Write about your experience below.

_____

_____

_____

_____

_____

_____

_____

_____

_____

_____

_____

_____

58. Sharing Sadness

Sometimes we feel better about being sad if we can share our sadness with someone else. We call the sharing of sadness **EMPATHY.**

Write about a time when you felt sad. Share your experience by reading it to a friend. Listen to your friend's experience of sadness.

_____

_____

_____

_____

_____

_____

_____

_____

_____

59. Easing Sadness for Others

What do you do when you know a friend or family member feels sad?

_____ try to talk to him/her about why he/she feels sad.

_____ talk to him/her about something else to take his/her mind off of being sad.

_____ leave him/her alone until he/she does not feel bad.

_____ do something nice for him/her.

_____ give him/her a gift, card, or note to make him/her feel less sad.

_____ other _____

_____

60. I Can Lessen Sadness

Find someone in your home, school, or neighborhood who is feeling sad. Choose one way to help him/her feel happier:

_____ talk to him/her about his/her sadness.

_____ spend time with him/her in an enjoyable activity.

_____ write him/her a note or a card, or make him/her a gift to help him/her feel less sad.

Discuss with your classmates what happened when you tried to help a sad person feel happier.

Summary: Feeling Sadness

The purpose of Part Three of this book was to assist you in describing your feelings of sadness. Summarize your thoughts in the space provided.

I feel sad when

_____

_____

_____

_____

When I am sad

_____

_____

_____

_____

Other people feel sad when

_____

_____

_____

_____

I can lessen my sadness by

_____

_____

_____

_____

I can lessen the sadness of others by

_____

_____

_____

_____

Check one:
After completing Part Three,

	Always	Usually	Sometimes	Seldom	Never
1. I feel sad	☐	☐	☐	☐	☐
2. I show that I am sad	☐	☐	☐	☐	☐
3. People close to me feel sad	☐	☐	☐	☐	☐
4. People close to me show when they are sad	☐	☐	☐	☐	☐

I think I am able to change my sadness to happiness:

☐ more

☐ less

☐ about the same

Name _____

Date _____

58

Feeling Lonely

Part Four:
to describe my feelings of loneliness.

Before beginning Part Four, **Feeling Lonely**, complete the following statements:

	Always	Usually	Sometimes	Seldom	Never
1. I feel lonely.	☐	☐	☐	☐	☐
2. I am by myself.	☐	☐	☐	☐	☐
3. It bothers me to be by myself.	☐	☐	☐	☐	☐
4. I like to be with people.	☐	☐	☐	☐	☐
5. I feel lonely in crowded places.	☐	☐	☐	☐	☐

Name _____

Date _____

61. Secret Saying

Decode the message. Read and discuss the meaning of the message with your classmates. (Note: Use the decoding grid to break the code. Each set of two numbers stands for a letter. For example, 12 stands for B because #1 of the row number and #2 of the column number meet at the letter B.)

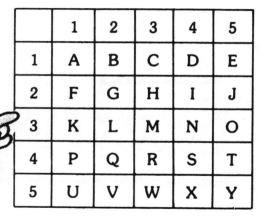

	1	2	3	4	5
1	A	B	C	D	E
2	F	G	H	I	J
3	K	L	M	N	O
4	P	Q	R	S	T
5	U	V	W	X	Y

45 23 15   45 24 33 15   45 35   12 15

— — —   — — — —   — —   — —

23 11 41 41 55   24 44   34 35 53

— — — — —   — —   — — —•

45 23 15   41 32 11 13 15   45 35   12 15

— — —   — — — — —   — —   — —

23 11 41 41 55   24 44   23 15 43 15

— — — — —   — —   — — — —•

45 23 15   53 11 55   45 35   12 15

— — —   — — —   — —   — —

23 11 41 41 55   24 44   45 35   33 11 31 15

— — — — —   — —   — —   — — — —

35 45 23 15 43 44   23 11 41 41 55

— — — — — —   — — — — —•

62. Describing Loneliness

Complete the sentences to describe your feelings of loneliness.

Example: Loneliness is waiting all day for a friend to call.

Loneliness is _____

_____

Loneliness is _____

_____

Loneliness is _____

_____

Discuss with your classmates and teacher a lonely feeling that you sometimes have. Add your description of loneliness to the "Loneliness is . . ." bulletin board in the classroom.

63. **Lonely Times**

Describe your feelings of loneliness in each of the following situations:·

I feel lonely at **home** when _____

_____

_____

I feel lonely at a **party** when _____

_____

_____

I feel lonely **with my friends** when _____

_____

_____

64. **From Loneliness to Belonging**

You can do something to change your feelings of loneliness to feelings of belonging. Choose one situation in Activity 63, and describe what you could do to change your feelings of loneliness to feelings of belonging at home, at school, at a party, or with your friends. Discuss with your teacher and classmates your plan for belonging.

65. Finding Loneliness

Below are five words often related to the feeling of loneliness. Find and circle these words in the word find.

depression

fright

shyness

boredom

withdrawal

W	I	T	H	D	R	A	W	A	L
A	J	B	D	E	W	E	F	R	Y
K	C	S	V	P	E	Q	X	H	G
U	U	B	O	R	E	D	O	M	Z
Z	T	L	I	E	G	H	M	Y	N
T	F	J	W	S	O	X	P	M	K
A	V	E	K	S	D	L	B	I	C
S	B	F	R	I	G	H	T	N	L
G	D	R	C	O	Q	F	P	H	O
E	S	H	Y	N	E	S	S	A	J

66. Finding Solutions to Loneliness

If you had a good friend with one of the feelings listed in Activity 65, what might you suggest for your friend to feel less lonely?

Problem: depression

Solution: _____

_____

_____

Problem: fright

Solution: _____

_____

_____

Problem: shyness

Solution: _____

_____

_____

Problem: boredom

Solution: _____

_____

_____

Problem: withdrawal

Solution: _____

_____

_____

67. Reasons for Loneliness

Listed below are some reasons why people might find themselves more lonely than they need be. Complete the sentences with the help of your classmates.

Examples:

Some people _____talk_____ more than they _____listen_____.
Some people _think of themselves_ more than they _think of others_.

1. Some people _____ more than they _____.

2. Some people _____ more than they _____.

3. Some people _____ more than they _____.

4. Some people _____ more than they _____.

5. Some people _____ more than they _____.

6. Some people _____ more than they _____.

7. Some people _____ more than they _____.

8. Some people _____ more than they _____.

68. Slice of the Pie

a. Divide the pie and label its pieces as to the main causes for loneliness in your life. Draw big pieces for major reasons for loneliness. Draw small pieces for minor reasons for loneliness.

b. Share your **biggest** piece of pie (your major **reason** for loneliness) with your **teacher**. Discuss reasons and solutions to **your** feelings of loneliness.

69. Alone with Myself

Do you ever enjoy being alone? _____

When do you like being by yourself? _____

_____

_____

_____

When do you not like being by yourself? _____

_____

_____

_____

_____

70. Alone or Together

Play a game of cards by yourself. Now play the same game of cards with a friend. Tell which game you enjoyed better and why.

_____

_____

_____

_____

_____

_____

71. Doing Things— Alone & Together

a. List five things you enjoy doing **alone**.

1. _____

_____

2. _____

_____

3. _____

_____

4. _____

_____

5. _____

_____

b. List five things you enjoy doing with **other people**.

1. _____

_____

2. _____

_____

3. _____

_____

4. _____

_____

5. _____

_____

c. Put a star (★) next to the four things listed above that you enjoy doing the **most.**

d. Check the one statement below that best describes you.

_____ I enjoy doing things **alone.**

_____ I enjoy doing things with **other people.**

_____ I enjoy doing things **alone** and with **other people** equally well.

72. Loneliness vs. Solitude

Discuss with your teacher and classmates the difference between loneliness and solitude. Write the difference below.

_____

_____

_____

_____

_____

_____

_____

73. Alone & Loving It

Write a poem called a cinquain, describing the peace, happiness, and·
relaxation of being alone in a special place doing something you like to do.
Write the name of this special place on the title of your poem. On the first
line, write two descriptive words that tell what the place looks like. On the
second line, write three positive words describing how you feel when you are
alone at this place. On the third and fourth lines, write a short phrase that
tells what you do when you are alone in this special place. On the last line,
write one word that best describes this place. Share your cinquain with
classmates.

74. Remedy for Loneliness

a)   When you are feeling lonely, what could you do to feel less lonely?

_____

_____

_____

_____

_____

b)   When someone is feeling lonely, what could you recommend so the person could feel less lonely?

_____

_____

_____

_____

_____

75. Eliminating Loneliness

a) Choose one or more of the actions described below to ease or eliminate loneliness for yourself and someone else.

_____ Write a letter to someone who would enjoy hearing from you.

_____ Call someone on the telephone who would like to talk with you.

_____ Spend lunch or recess time with a classmate who usually works alone on projects.

_____ Work with someone in your class who usually works alone on projects.

_____ Visit a nursing home and spend some time with an elderly person.

_____ (Write and carry out your own action for eliminating loneliness.)

_____

_____

_____

b) Describe one of your experiences checked above.

_____

_____

_____

Summary: Feeling Lonely

The purpose of Part Four of this book was to assist you in identifying and changing your feelings of loneliness. Summarize your thoughts in the space provided.

Name _____

Date _____

I am lonely when

_____
_____
_____

Some remedies for my loneliness are

_____
_____
_____

Some things I like to do by myself are

_____
_____
_____
_____
_____

Some things I like to do with others are

_____
_____
_____
_____
_____

Check one: After completing Part Four, I feel lonely:

☐ more

☐ less

☐ about the same

Check one: After completing this book, I understand my feelings of love, happiness, sadness, and loneliness:

☐ more

☐ less

☐ about the same

Final Summary:

Answer the following statements after completing the activities on feeling love, happy, sad, and lonely.

		Always	Usually	Sometimes	Seldom	Never
FEELING LOVE	1. I love myself.					
	2. I love people.					
	3. I love animals.					
	4. I show my love for people.					
	5. People show their love for me.					
FEELING HAPPY	6. I am happy.					
	7. I show my happiness.					
	8. Other people are happy.					
	9. Other people show their happiness.					
FEELING SAD	10. I feel sad.					
	11. I show that I feel sad.					
	12. People close to me feel sad.					
	13. People close to me show when they are sad.					
FEELING LONELY	14. I feel lonely.					
	15. I am by myself.					
	16. It bothers me to be by myself.					
	17. I like to be with people.					
	18. I feel lonely in crowded places.					

Name _____ Date _____

After completing this book, I understand my feelings of love, happiness, sadness, and loneliness: _____ more, _____ less, _____ about the same

NOTES